A First Look at Monsters

by Emma Carlson-Berne

BUMBA BOOKS™

LERNER PUBLICATIONS ◆ MINNEAPOLIS

To Finn

Note to Educators

Throughout this book, you'll find critical-thinking questions. These can be used to engage young readers in thinking critically about the topic and in using the text and photos to do so.

Lerner Publications Company
An imprint of Lerner Publishing Group, Inc.
241 First Avenue North
Minneapolis, MN 55401 USA

For reading levels and more information, look up this title at www.lernerbooks.com.

Main body text set in Helvetica Textbook Com Roman.
Typeface provided by Linotype AG.

Designer: Lauren Cooper
Lerner team: Martha Kranes

Library of Congress Cataloging-in-Publication Data

Names: Carlson-Berne, Emma, 1979– author.
Title: A first look at monsters / Emma Carlson-Berne.
Description: Minneapolis : Lerner Publications, [2021] | Series: Bumba books- fantastic creatures | Includes bibliographical references and index. | Audience: Ages 4–7 | Audience: Grades K–1 | Summary: "Readers learn about the stories ancient peoples used to tell about three monsters: griffins, krakens, and centaurs."— Provided by publisher.
Identifiers: LCCN 2019042921 (print) | LCCN 2019042922 (ebook) | ISBN 9781541596832 (library binding) | ISBN 9781541599758 (ebook)
Subjects: LCSH: Monsters—Juvenile literature. | Griffins—Juvenile literature. | Kraken—Juvenile literature. | Centaurs—Juvenile literature.
Classification: LCC GR825 .B487 2021 (print) | LCC GR825 (ebook) | DDC 001.944—dc23

LC record available at https://lccn.loc.gov/2019042921
LC ebook record available at https://lccn.loc.gov/2019042922

Manufactured in the United States of America
1-47789-48229-11/20/2019

Table of Contents

Monsters! 4

Parts of Monsters 22

Picture Glossary 23

Read More 24

Index 24

Monsters!

Monsters are not real. But imagining them can be fun!

Can you picture a monster that is half eagle and half lion? It's a griffin!

Ancient Greeks imagined a monster called a griffin. It had big wings. In some stories, it guarded gold treasure. It was very fierce.

Imagine a monster with a horse's body and a person's head. That's a centaur!

Ancient Greeks thought monsters called centaurs hid in forests. In stories, centaurs had strong hooves. They were wild and tough.

What color might a centaur be?

Sailors thought there were huge sea monsters called krakens. Krakens had many tentacles. Their bodies could be as big as an island in some stories!

Ancient people often thought monsters were real. They sometimes found dinosaur fossils. They thought they had found griffin bones.

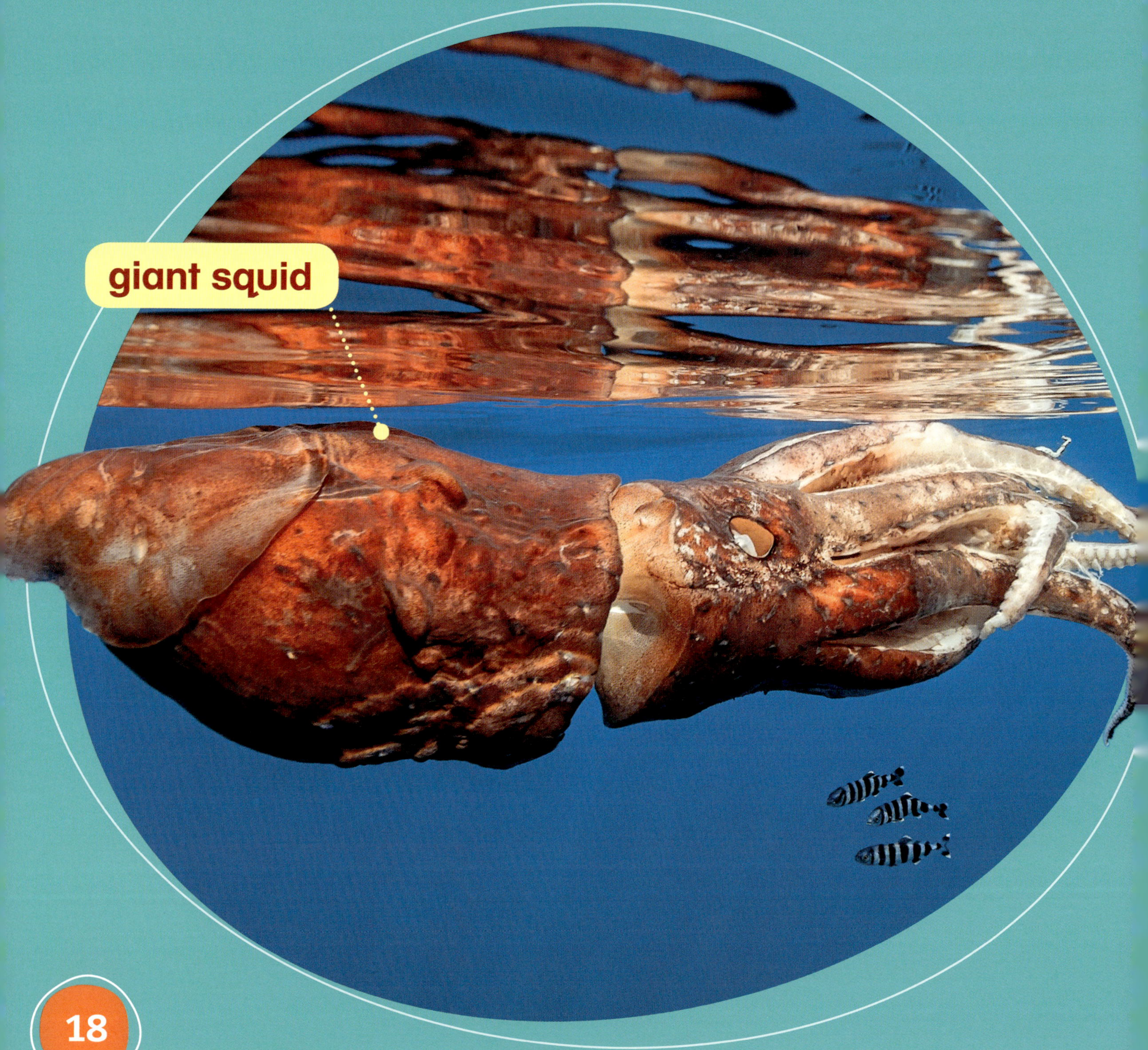
giant squid

Sailors sometimes saw real giant squid. They imagined krakens.

What other real sea animal might look like a kraken?

We can enjoy stories about monsters,

even if they are just pretend!

Parts of Monsters

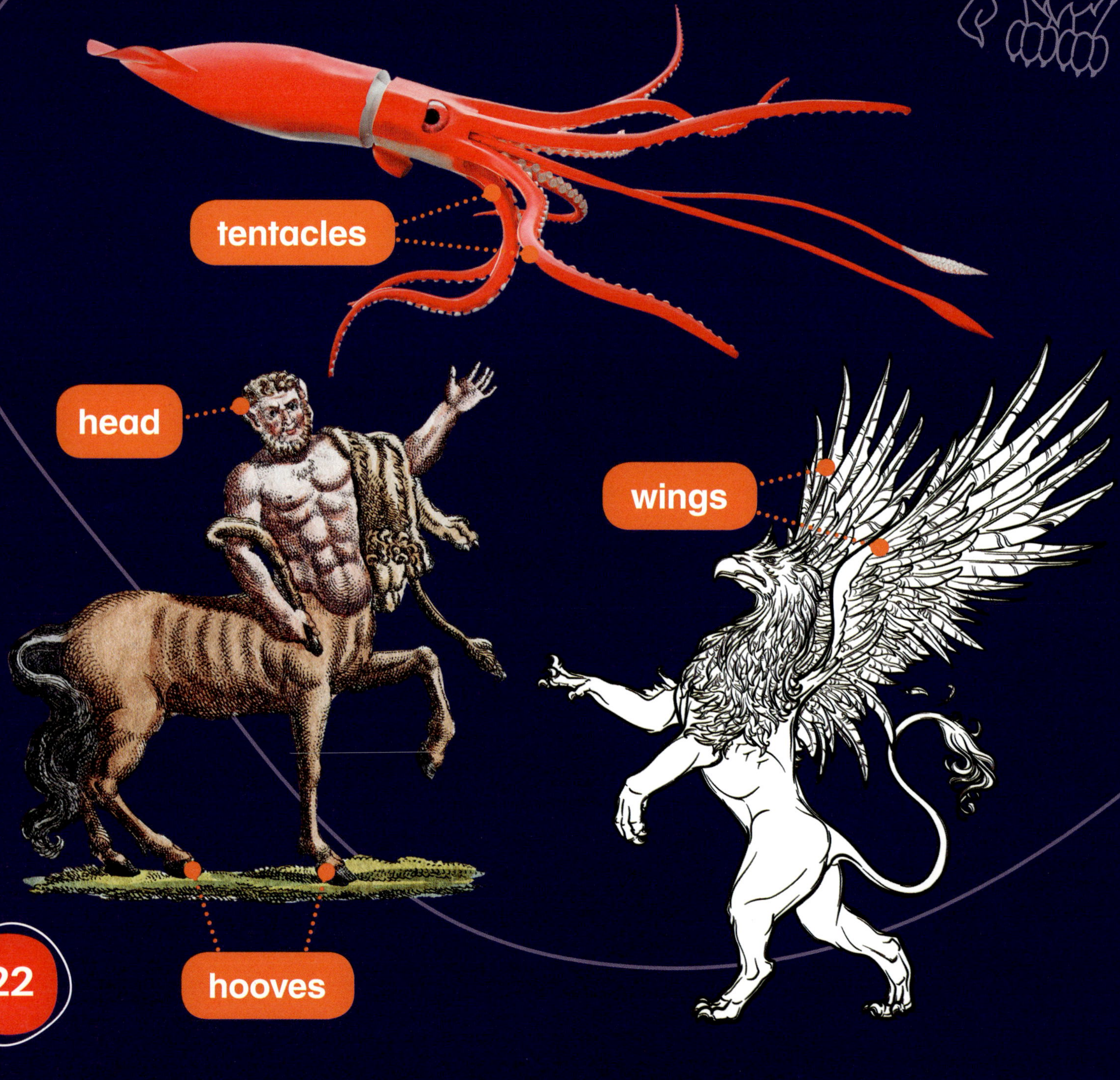

Picture Glossary

imagining

pretending something in your mind

squid

an ocean animal that has ten tentacles

tentacles

flexible arms

treasure

something valuable such as money or jewels

Read More

Carlson-Berne, Emma. *A First Look at Dragons*. Minneapolis: Lerner Publications, 2021.

Felix, Rebecca. *Fossils*. Minneapolis: Sandcastle, 2018.

Sommer, Nathan. *Squids*. Minneapolis: Bellwether Media, 2018.

Index

bones, 16

eagle, 7

horse, 10

lion, 7

sailors, 15, 19

squid, 19

treasure, 8

Photo Credits

Images used with the permission of: yulkapopkova/Getty Images, pp. 5, 23; duncan1890/Getty Images, p. 6; alexsol/Getty Images, pp. 9, 23; Macrovector/Shutterstock.com, p. 11; sSplajn/iStock/Getty Images, p. 12; Xarlyxa/iStock/Getty Images, p. 14; Yicai/iStock/Getty Images, p. 17; by wildestanimal/Getty Images, p. 18; Maskot/Getty Images, p. 20; abadonian/iStock/Getty Images, p. 22; Olaf Kruger/Getty Images, p. 22; Anton_Tokarev/iStock/Getty Images, p. 22; Nicolas Ayer/EyeEm/Getty Images, p. 23.

Cover image: ratpack223/Getty Images.